BEST OF
SPA DESIGN

Imprint
The Deutsche Bibliothek is registering this publication in the Deutsche Nationalbibliogra-
phie; detailed bibliographical information can be found on the internet at http://dnb.ddb.de

ISBN 978-3-938780-69-5
© 2009 by Verlagshaus Braun
www.verlagshaus-braun.de

1st edition 2009

Editorial staff: Annika Schulz
Translation: Stephen Roche, Hamburg
Graphic concept: Michaela Prinz

BEST OF
SPA DESIGN

BRAUN

relax!

Preface

There are social trends that are quickly reflected in the prevailing architectural style. The new joy of cooking, for example, has led to kitchens being increasingly designed as open spaces today. Within the past few years, a rethinking process took place in this area that substantially altered the view of a functional part of the home. In the bathroom sector a similar trend seems to be taking place that is expected to increase in the near future. The interesting aspect of this trend is the correlation between public and private bathing areas. This is mainly the reason why the fashionable term SPA has become the synonym for restorative relaxation – increasingly also in the privacy of the home.

However, the frequently stated belief that the word spa is a Latin acronym – sanus per aquam (health through water) – is only an illusion since neither the sources nor the rules of Latin grammar support such a conclusion. Instead the symbolic value of the word actually derives from the Belgian bathing resort of Spa, which was already frequented by British tourists in the 16th century. Yet antiquity is an interesting starting point for studying the culture of bathing. The Roman Thermae were public places and water a precious commodity that was fetched via aqueducts. The link between hygiene and sufficient water supply was one of the basic pillars of the imperium romanum. In the Middle Ages, public bath houses were the place in which most people came in contact with running water. Crusaders had brought the concept and the construction plans along with them from the Middle East. However, religious prudery, the spread of syphilis and, last but not least,

the great bubonic plague epidemics resulted in the shutting down of most bath houses. From then on, especially among feudal circles, personal hygiene was reduced to the use of perfumes.

It was not until the 19th century that new hygienic insights led to a revival of public baths. This was followed by the increased privatization of baths. Gaining in strength, the bourgeoisie added bathrooms as a representative architectural element to their homes, creating a new functional room. Until the period of promoterism many urban houses at least featured a common bathroom in the hallway. Individualization progressed as people were now eager to construct a separate bathroom in each residential unit. Those who had plenty of space at their disposal even managed to install a guest toilet or guest bathroom. This progressed into the assignment of separate bathing areas to each person in the household, where possible. Whether the efforts include installing master bathrooms, parent and children bathrooms or simple dual bathroom sinks, all have one aim in common – turning the bathroom into an individual area of expression and retreat. This way, in its architectural evolution from a public to a private space, the bathroom developed into the perfect symbol of cocooning.

As a result of the recent wellness movement, an exciting observation can be made at this point. Increasingly, public bathing institutions that for a long time only drudged along as boring swimming halls are gaining in popularity. Spruced up by architects and designers, they shine as new spa temples that not only revive the ritual character of bathing during antiquity but also include Middle Eastern and oriental influences. This way, they not only define a new public function for the bathing space but also act as ideals and models for the design of many private bathrooms.

Bathrooms in homes increasingly feature an open design while the choice of materials has expanded. The bathroom as a space is given more importance in the planning stage. Previously, bathrooms were frequently located on the interior, while today daylight illumination is almost compulsory. The number of manufacturers of bathroom furniture, faucets and ceramics is also constantly increasing. New materials and manufacturing techniques allow, for example, the use of tiles with unusual dimensions or sinks made of composite materials that can be molded in any shape. This way, they once again constitute cultic vessels for the matter whose specific characteristics enable life on earth – water. At $0°$ Celsius it turns into ice, at $4°$ it reaches its highest liquid density – a characteristics that not only ensures the survival of fish. Hot-blooded, our body temperature is around $37°$, and finally at $100°$, water evaporates into steam.

Far-Eastern motifs combined with **selected** materials create a **peaceful** atmosphere

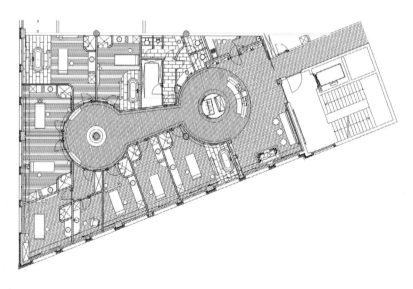

An **open design** combined with a **freestanding** element have created a **bathroom** that is **spacious yet simple**

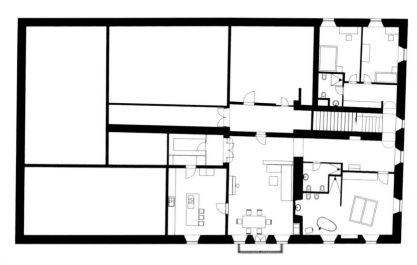

BATHHOUSE

Privacy and **secrecy** are **combined** with an **open landscape** of **water** in all forms

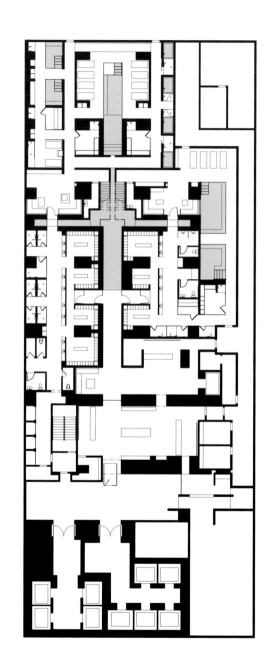

CHILDREN 12 YEARS OF AGE
OR YOUNGER MUST BE
ACCOMPANIED BY AN ADULT.
THE MAXIMUM RECOMMENDED
TIME FOR SUCH CHILDREN TO
USE THE SPA IS 10 MINUTES.

CAPACITY   DIAL 911   CAUTION

MEDICAL·POLICE·FIRE
FOR LOCATION · FRONT DESK

17 MAXIMUM NUMBER OF PEOPLE
ALLOWED IN THE SPA AT ONE TIME

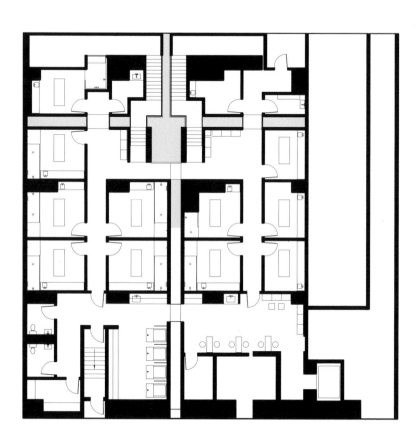

Creating an atmosphere of tranquility

Bathroom in Velp | Velp | Dirkjan Broekhuizen Interieurarchitect BNI

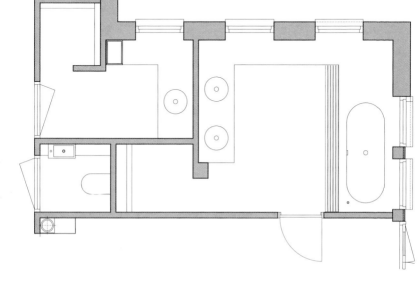

Stucco, cement panels, wallpaper and **wood** provide **distinct** individual atmospheres

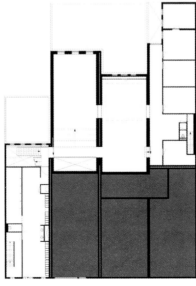

DeWispelaere | Herne | Venlet Interior Architecture bvba

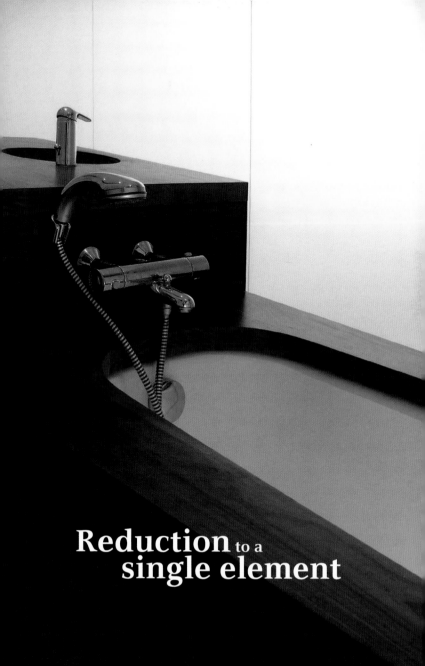

Reduction to a
single element

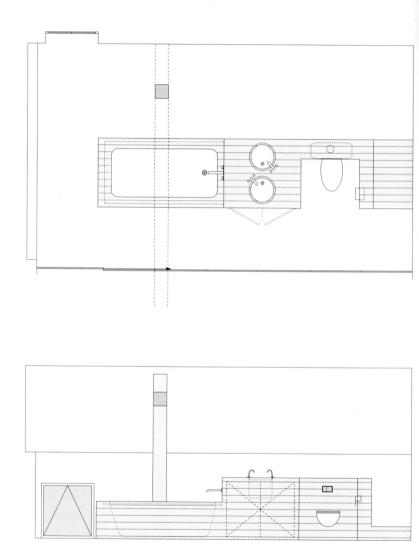

A **colorful** installation to
relax body and **soul**

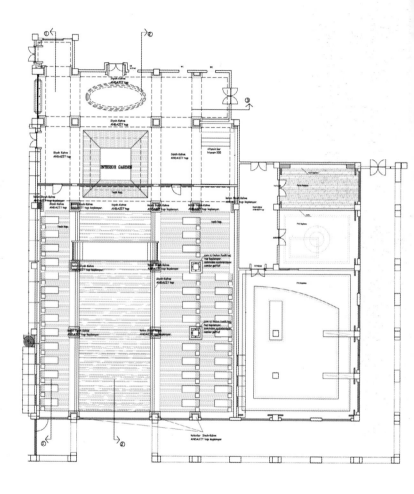

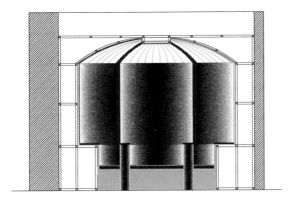

A-A KESİT

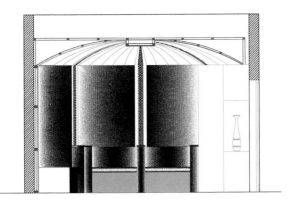

B-B KESİT

Dornbracht Elemental Spa | Frankfurt / Main | Meiré und Meiré

Combining **physicality** and **water** with **archaic architecture**

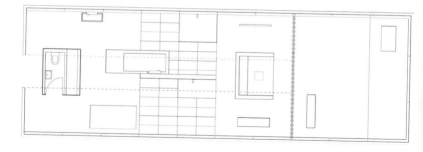

The **only elements** employed here are **water, stone** and **light**

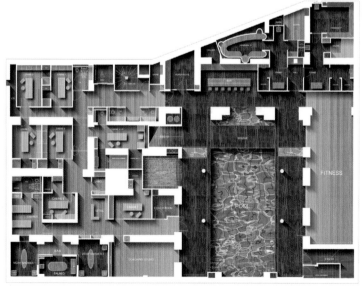

Geleen Bath | Amsterdam | Otello Gatto

Corton rust-finish tiles
combined with **mosaic**

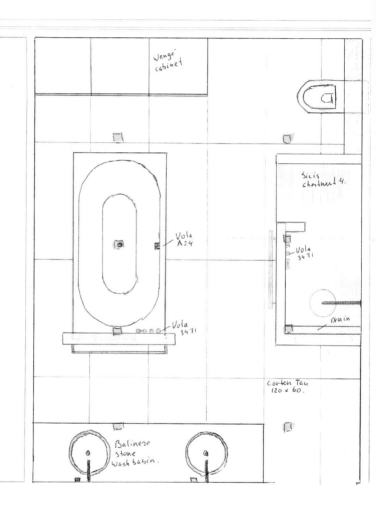

Wengé cabinet

Vola A24

Vola 3471

Sicis chestnut 4.

Vola 3471

Drain

Corten Tau 120 x 60.

Balinese stone washbasin.

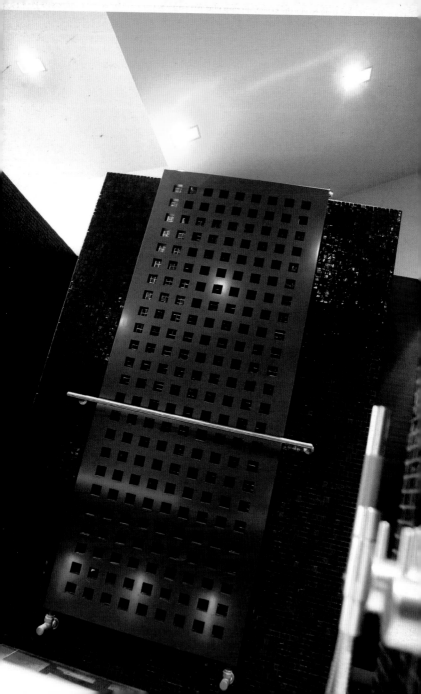

98 | **Hamam Trafo** | Baden | integrales Planungsteam Ushi Tamborriello, Innenarchiotektur & Szenenbild

This **Turkish spa** creates an ambience of **earthy mysticism** with surfaces in different **shades of gray** and **green** and green-lit pools

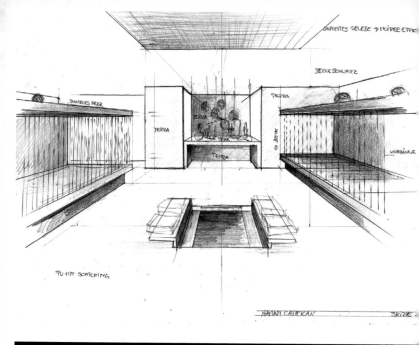

DARKLES HOLZ

TERRA

TERRA

TERRA

TERRA

TEAK

CO TERA

TERRA

DARKLES HOLZ

GOSPELLES GELEBE D'ICIREE EFFIC

JECKE SCHWARZ

VORHÄNGE

PUNT SCATCHING

HATAN CASHERAN   SKIZE

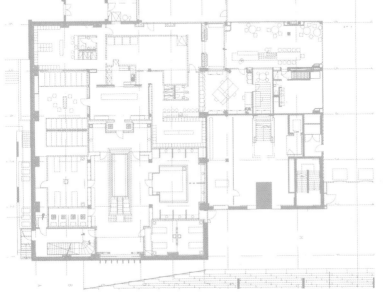

108 | **Health Center Lanserhof** | Lans near Innsbruck | D E SIGNSTUDIO Regina Dahmen-Ingenhoven

Soft colors, shapes and materials, **inviting** visitors to **relax** and **regain** their strength

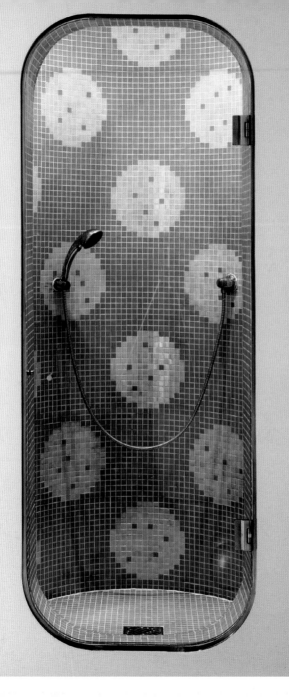

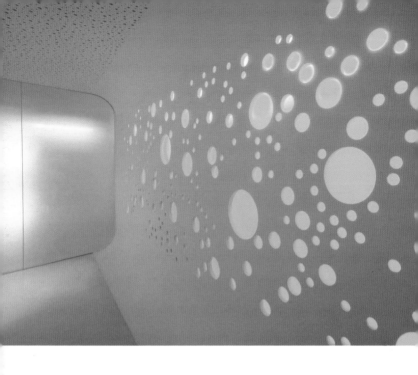

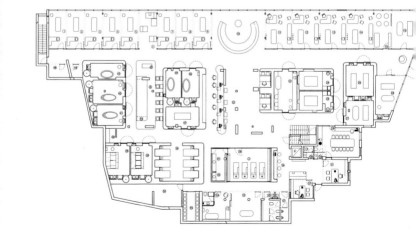

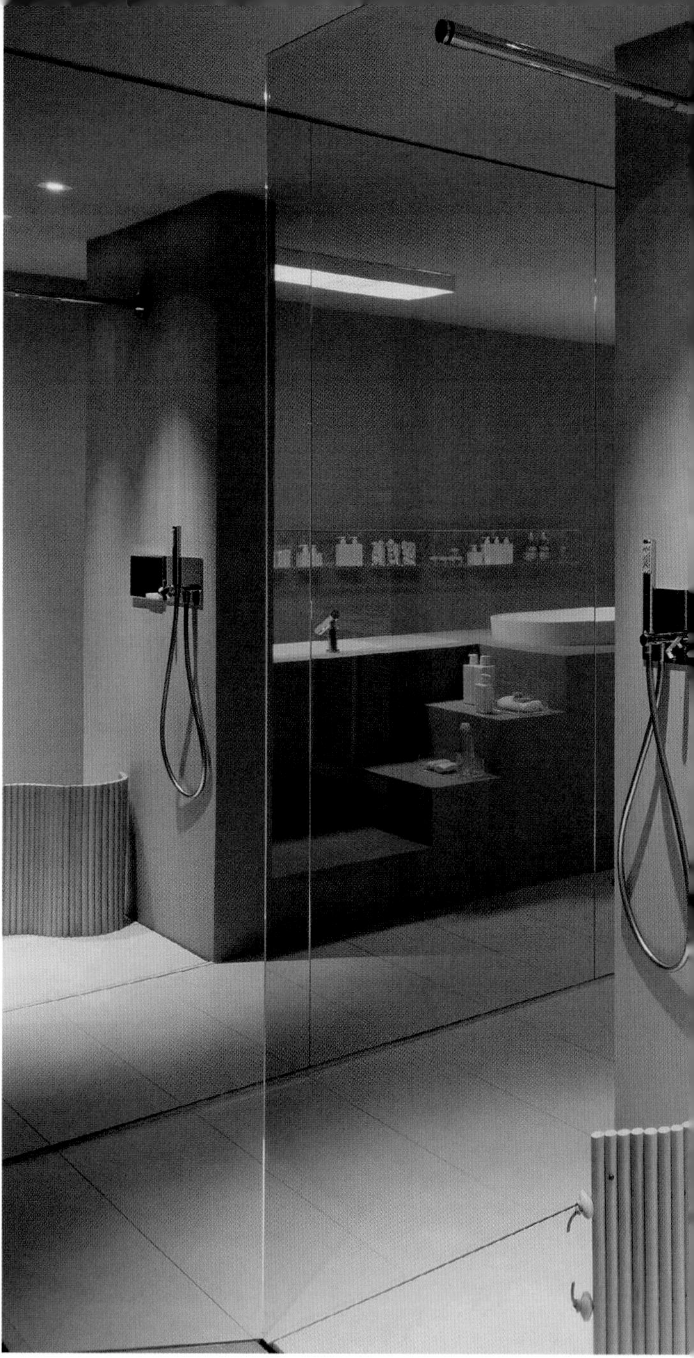

A **sequence** of
seven settings

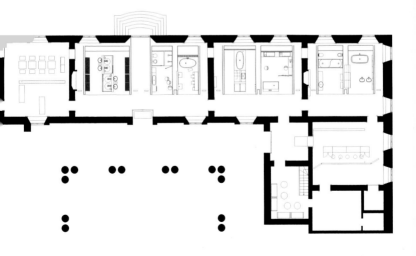

The **light changes** from bright **yellow-orange** in the morning to **dark blue** at night

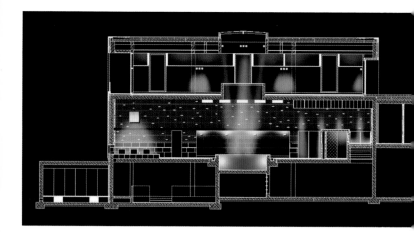

This **hybrid bath-** and **bedroom** allows for **double** functional **occupancy**

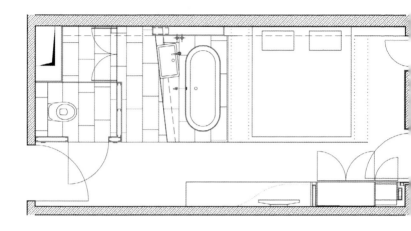

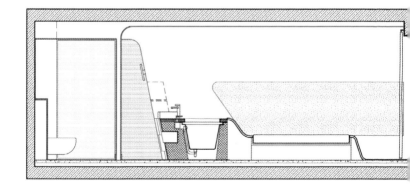

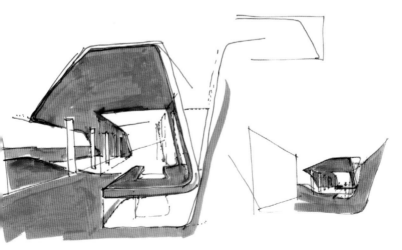

146 | **Kaufman Loft Bath** | New York | Studios Rinaldi

White Thasos **marble mosaic tiles** are combined with **terrazzo floor tiles**

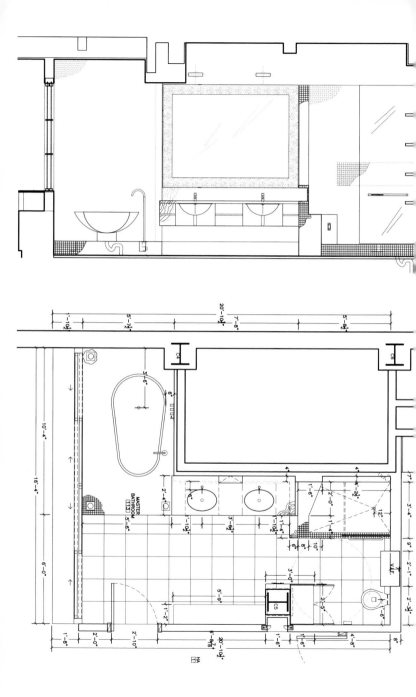

MASTER
BATHROOM
[11]

Kinuta Stone Spa | Tokyo | Megumi Matsubara & Hiroi Ariyama

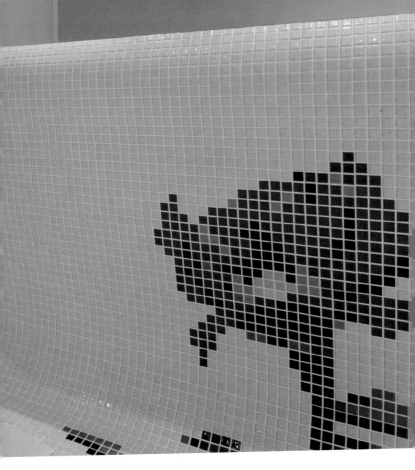

This **space creates** a clean and uncluttered **environment** that **draw** its users **into** deep relaxation

Stone Spa

staff room

cooldown room

waiting room

reception

powder space

balcony

changeroom

entrance

fire exit

shower room

massage room

Kusaba Apartment | Oita | Takao Shiotsuka Atelier

Concrete and glass walls create a strong yet open space

166 | **La Réserve Genève Hotel & Spa** | Bellevue | Jacques Garcia

Here is a **rich, luxurious** and **sophisticated** jungle **design** scheme

174 | **Labo Day Spa** | Zurich | Aroma Productions AG

Delicate **composition** of **natural** materials and **fine** colors

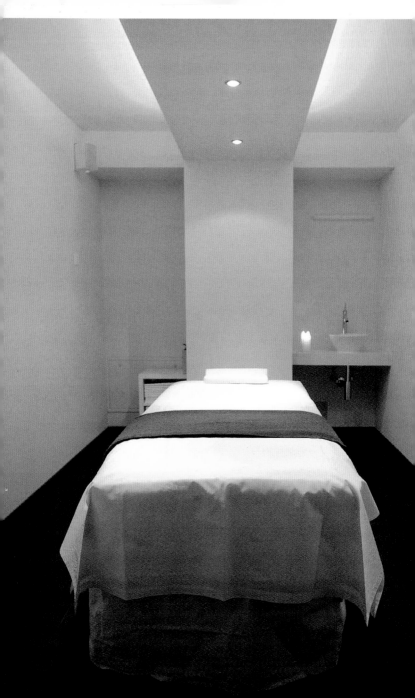

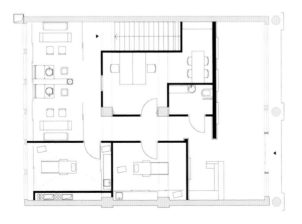

Liquidrom | Berlin | gmp – Architekten von Gerkan, Marg und Partner

Light and sound
define the atmosphere
of this space

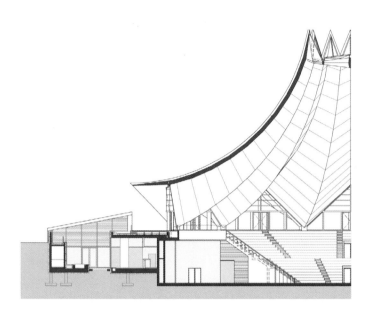

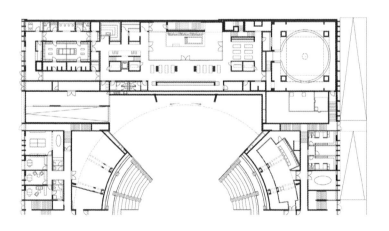

Both **bath** and **shower** **facilities** incorporate the **bright-blue floor**

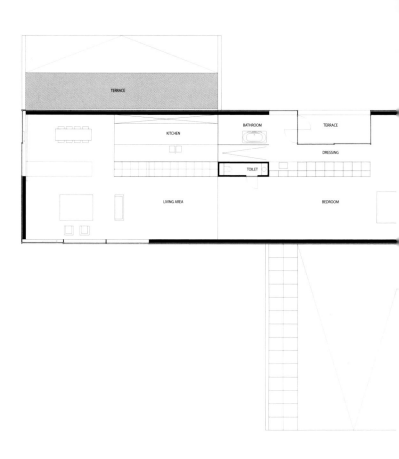

TERRACE

KITCHEN

BATHROOM

TERRACE

DRESSING

TOILET

LIVING AREA

BEDROOM

Loft Bathroom | Fulda | BUB architekten

A **spacious shower** and **isolated tub** combined with **compact** materials

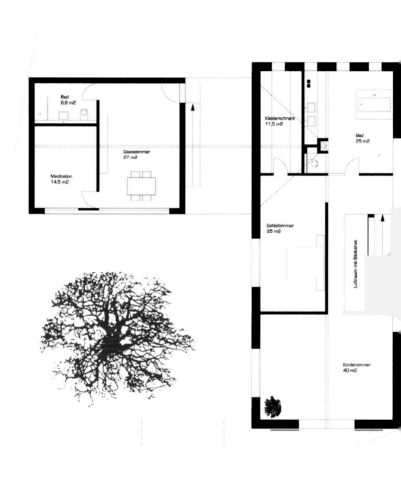

This design **uses zinc** fittings, colorful **teak motifs** and **Bisazza mosaic**

210 | **Lute Suites** | Amstelveen | Marcel Wanders Studio

McCarthy Residence | Sydney | stephen varady architecture

Exploring the potential
of glass as a modern
construction material

Designed to **manifest** the
Swedish ritual
of **sauna** baths

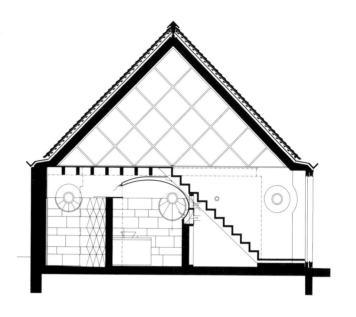

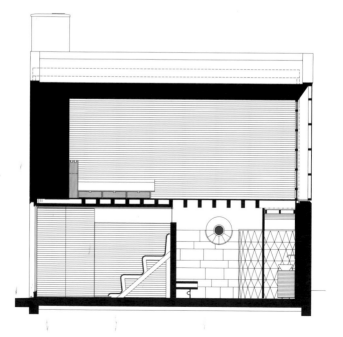

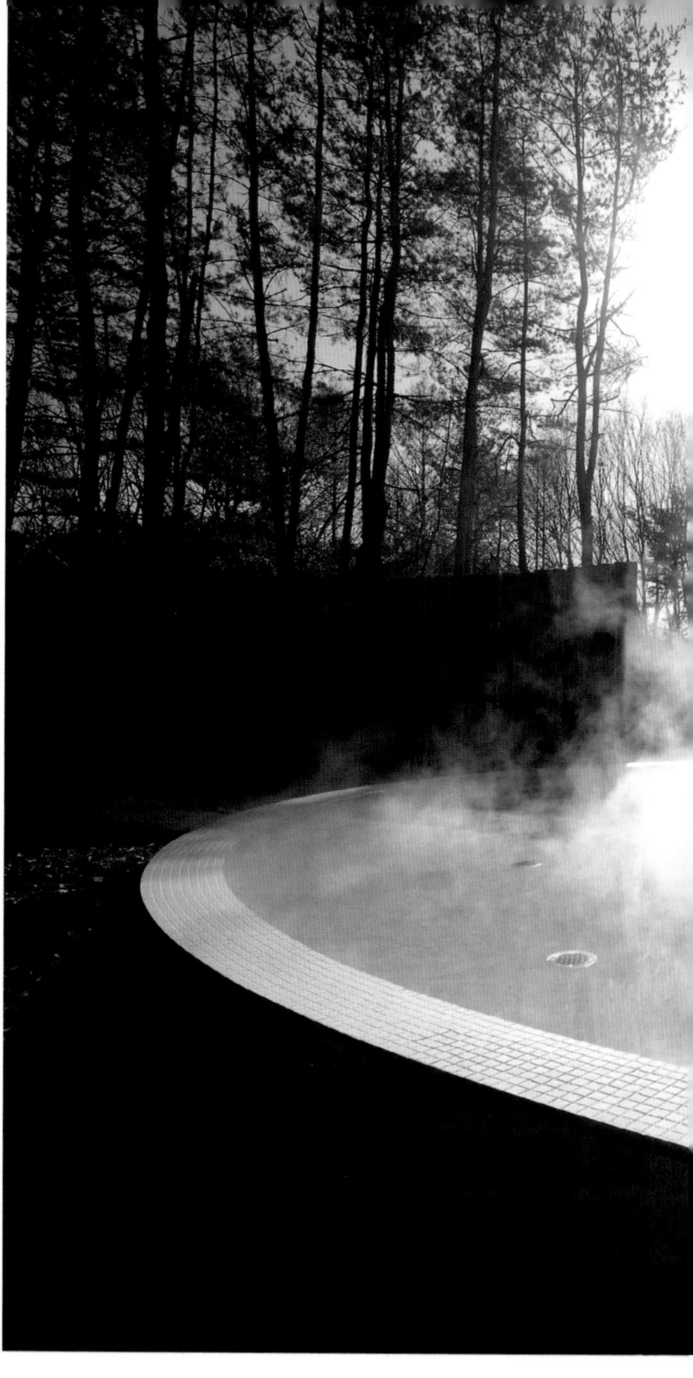

This spa offers **year-round**
bathing in a
sylvan setting

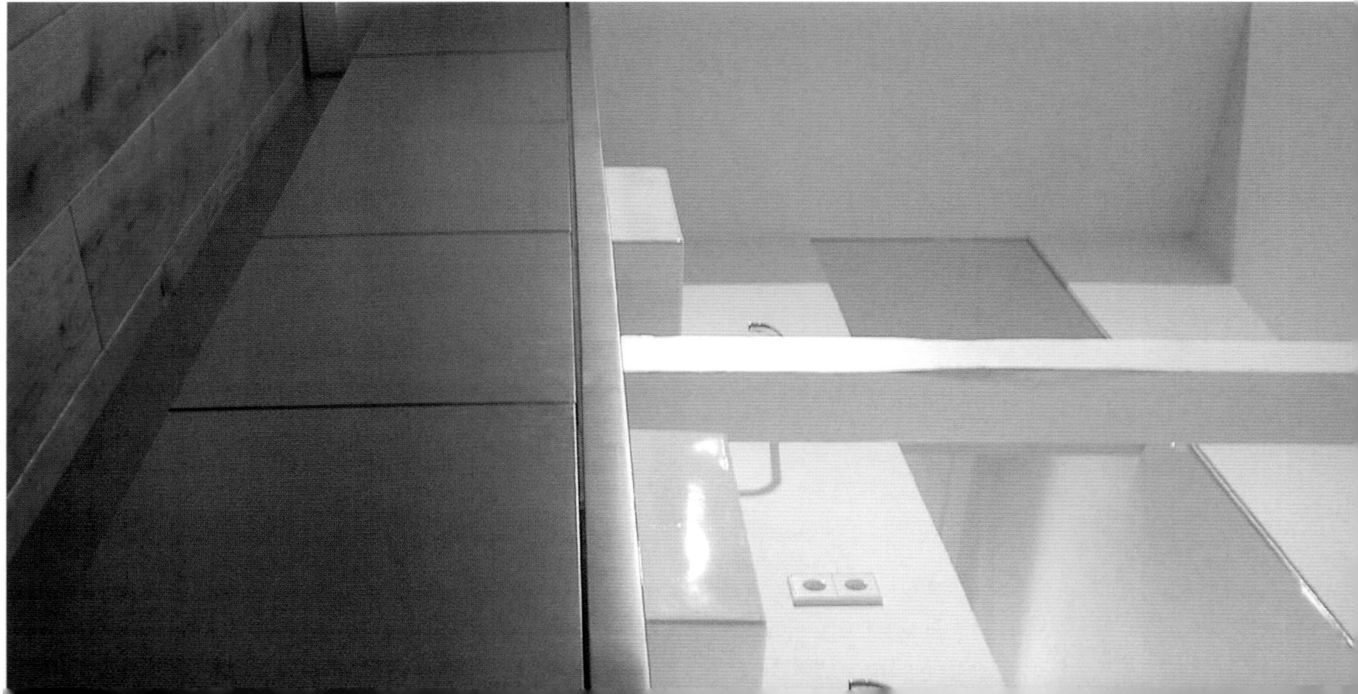

A **bathroom** that **acts** as an **open relaxation zone** between living and sleeping area

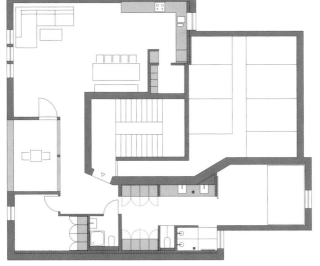

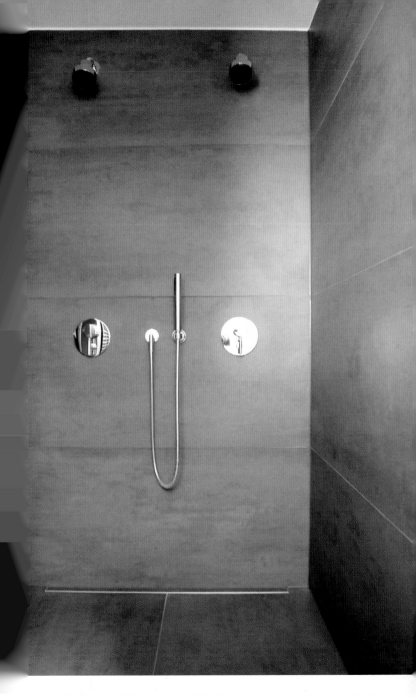

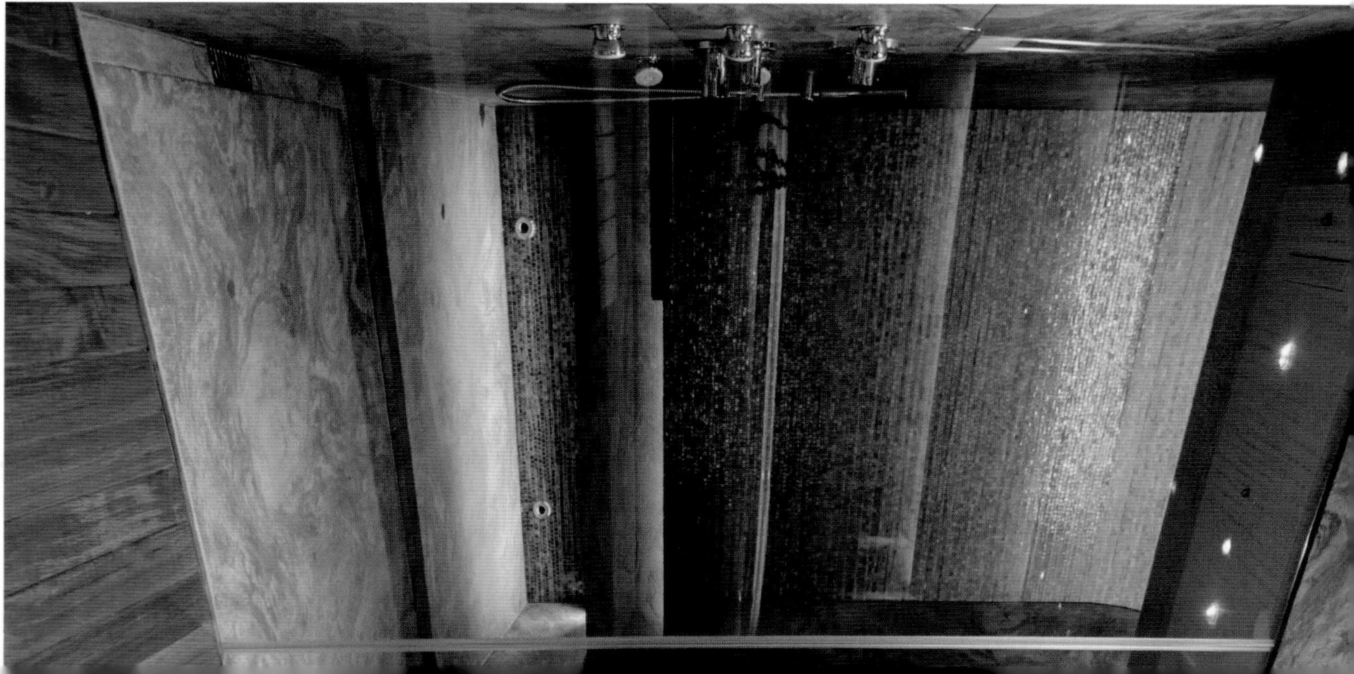

he harmonious design offers an excellent **indoor environment** coupled with **uperb functionality**

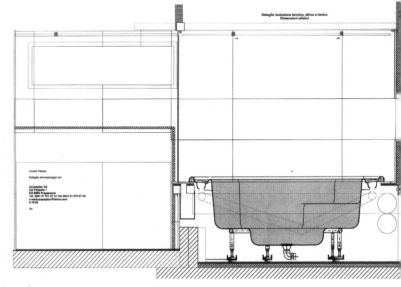

Dettaglio isolazione termico, idrico e fonico
Dimensioni effettivi

Locale Fitness

Dettaglio idromassaggio est

Acquaplan SA
Via Prédelle 1
CH-6983 Pregassona
Tel. 0041 91 971 31 31 Fax 0041 91 972 37 56
e-mail acquaplan@bluino.com
5.10.95

Ae

A very **small bathroom** with a **spacious feeling**

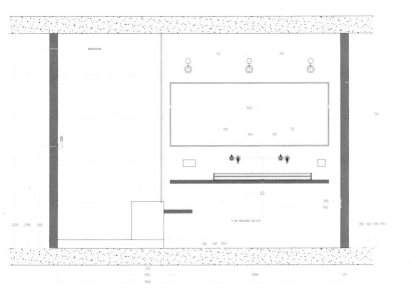

750   750

945

900   500   500   720

TO BE MEASURED ON SITE

350
950

2530   2350   1200

800 1000 1080 1950

600   450   550

400
1350
5962

2386   120

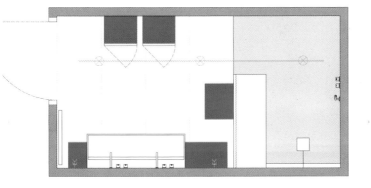

Special materials, strong colors and indirect light create a relaxing atmosphere

Puls5 | Zurich | Ushi Tamborriello Innenarchitektur & Szenenbild | Oberholzer & Brüschweiler Architekten

Refurbishment of a Bathroom | Cologne | Seiten_Ansicht

Detailed **style** with
marble cladding

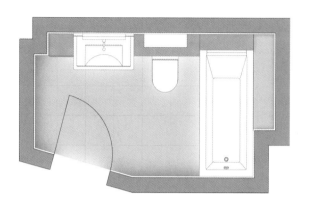

Regatta Condominium | New York | Leopoldo Rosati Architecture

Painted canvases provide depth and artistic allure

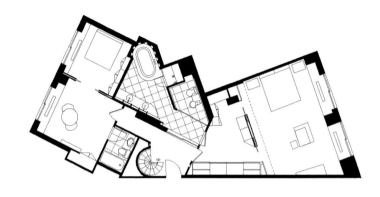

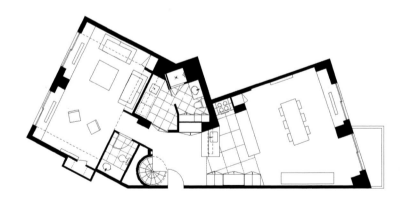

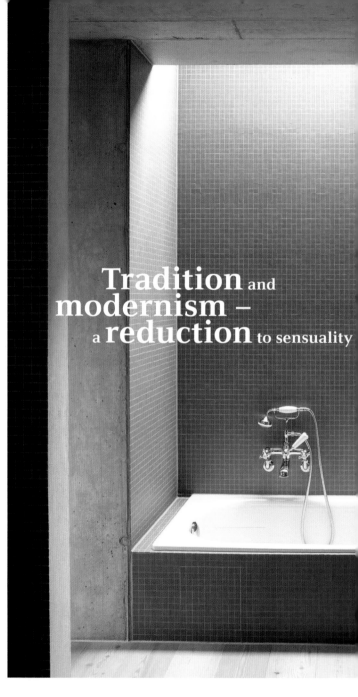

Tradition and
modernism –
a reduction to sensuality

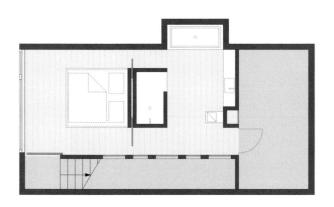

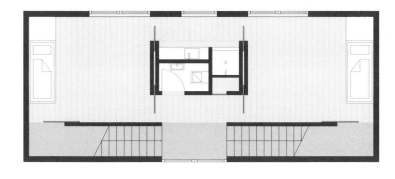

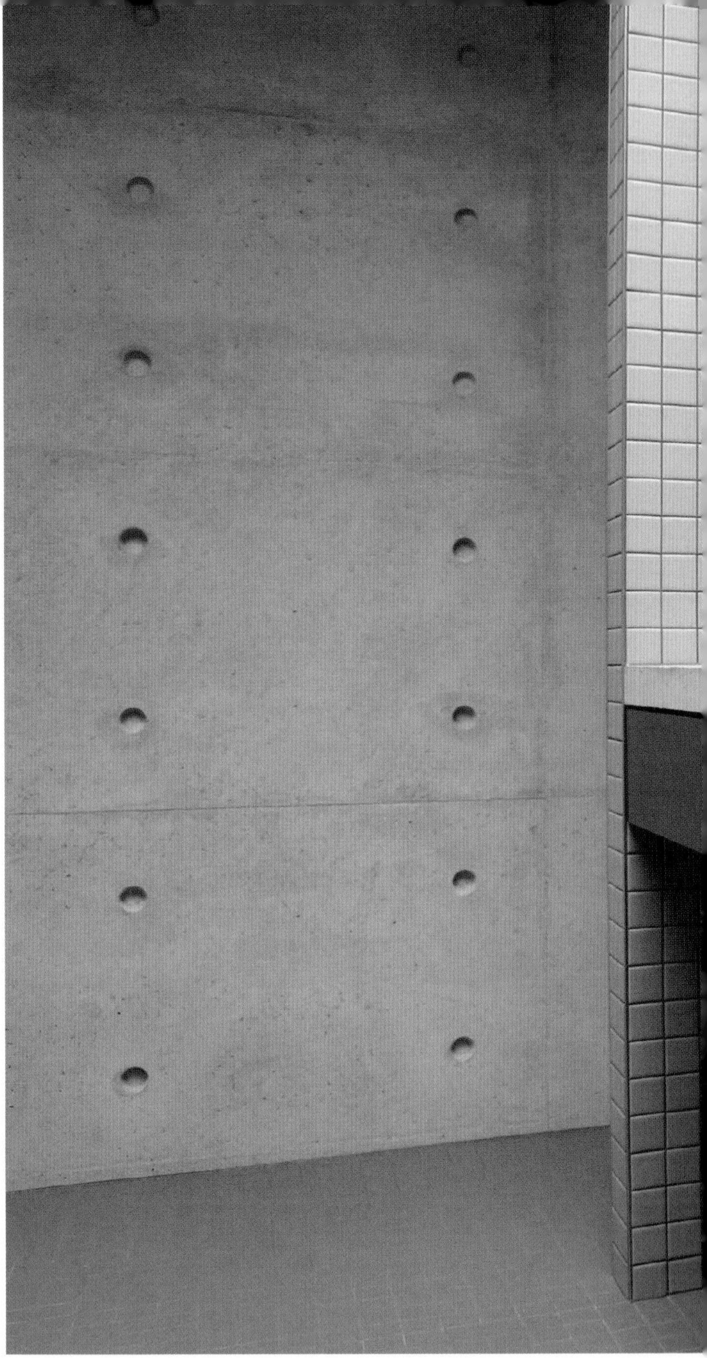

The **concrete structure** creates a **sublime mood**

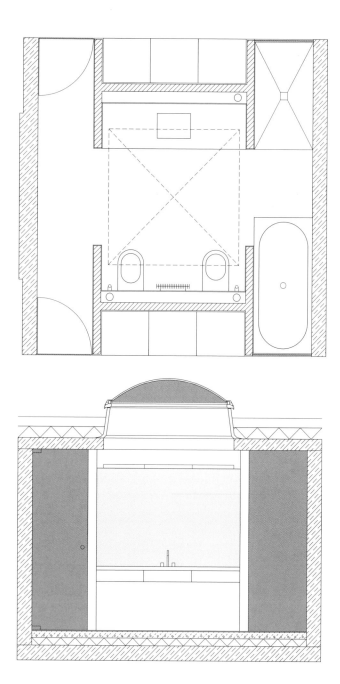

Inviting nature
into the home

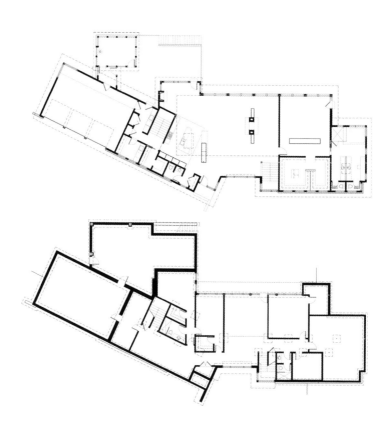

Silver Rain a La Prairie Spa | Grand Cayman | Carl D'Aquino & Francine Monaco
of D'Aquino Monaco

The guests are **surrounded** by the **comforting aura** of **water** in all its **states**

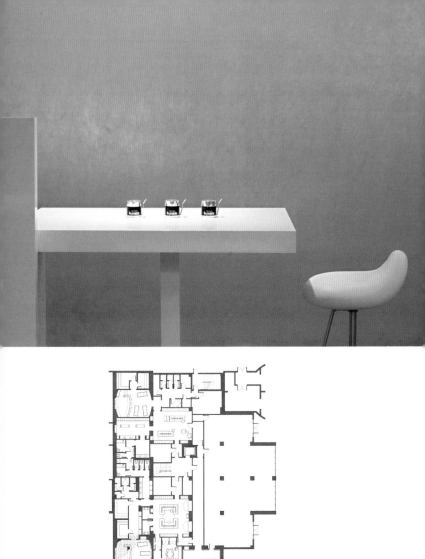
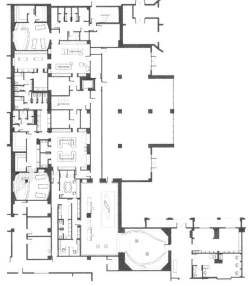

Spa Barn | Nakenstorf near Neukloster | Nalbach + Nalbach | Hon. Prof. Johanne Nalbach

The **bath area** plays with the elements **fire, water and earth**

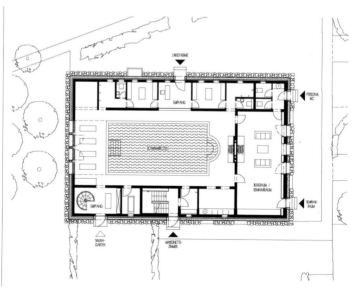

336 | **Spa Wolfsburg** | Wolfsburg | Büro Wehberg

This **spa** consciously employs a
minimalist style
and **pure elements**

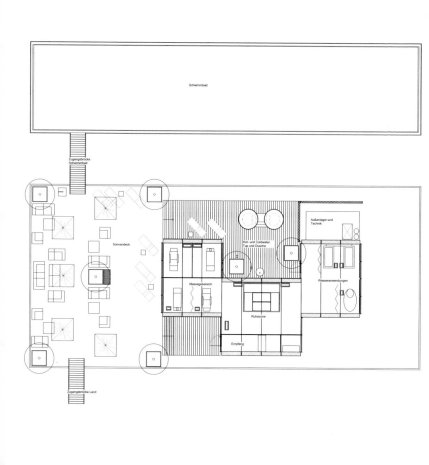

Schwimmbad

Zugangsbrücke
Schwimmbad

Sonnendeck

Außenlager und
Technik

Hot- und Coldwater
Tup und Dusche

Massagebereich

Wasseranwendungen

Ruhezone

Empfang

Zugangsbrücke Land

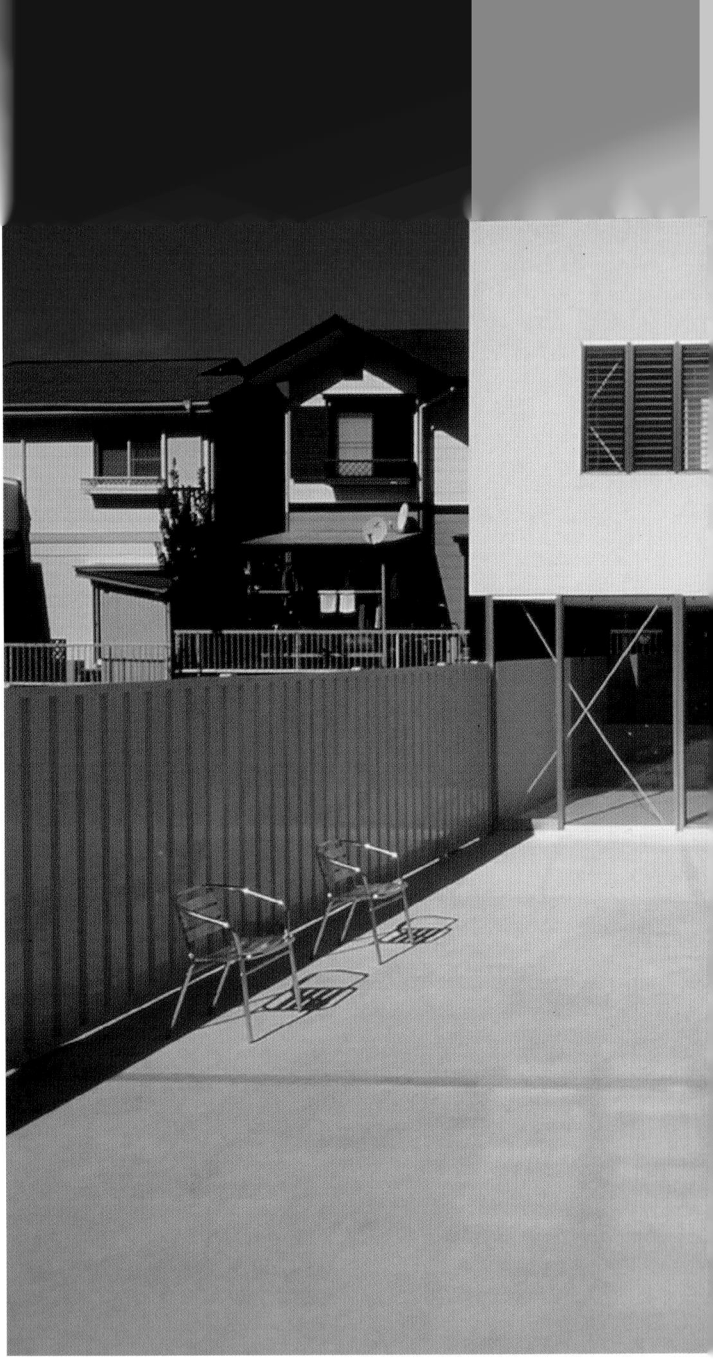

This is **modern take** on **Japanese Zen design**

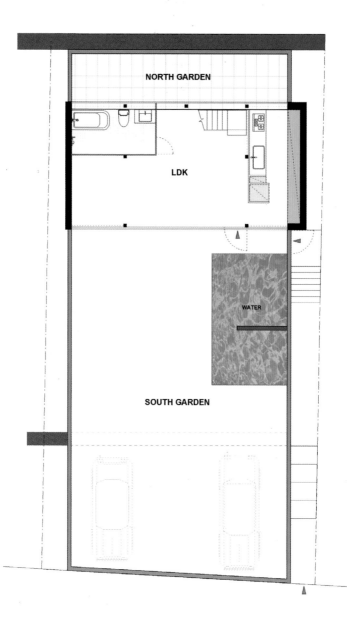

NORTH GARDEN

LDK

WATER

SOUTH GARDEN

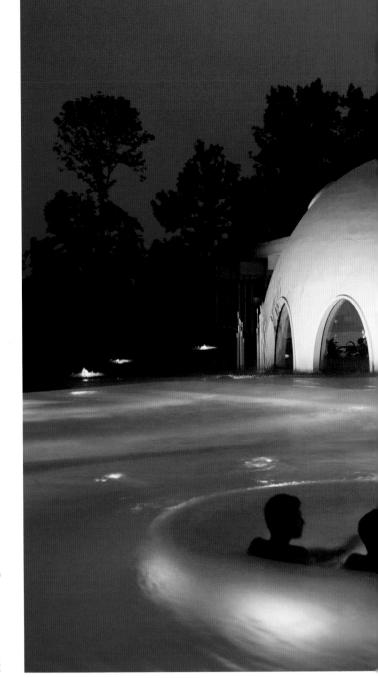

This spa offers **spacious relaxation** areas and a **choice of pools,** baths and **Jacuzzis**

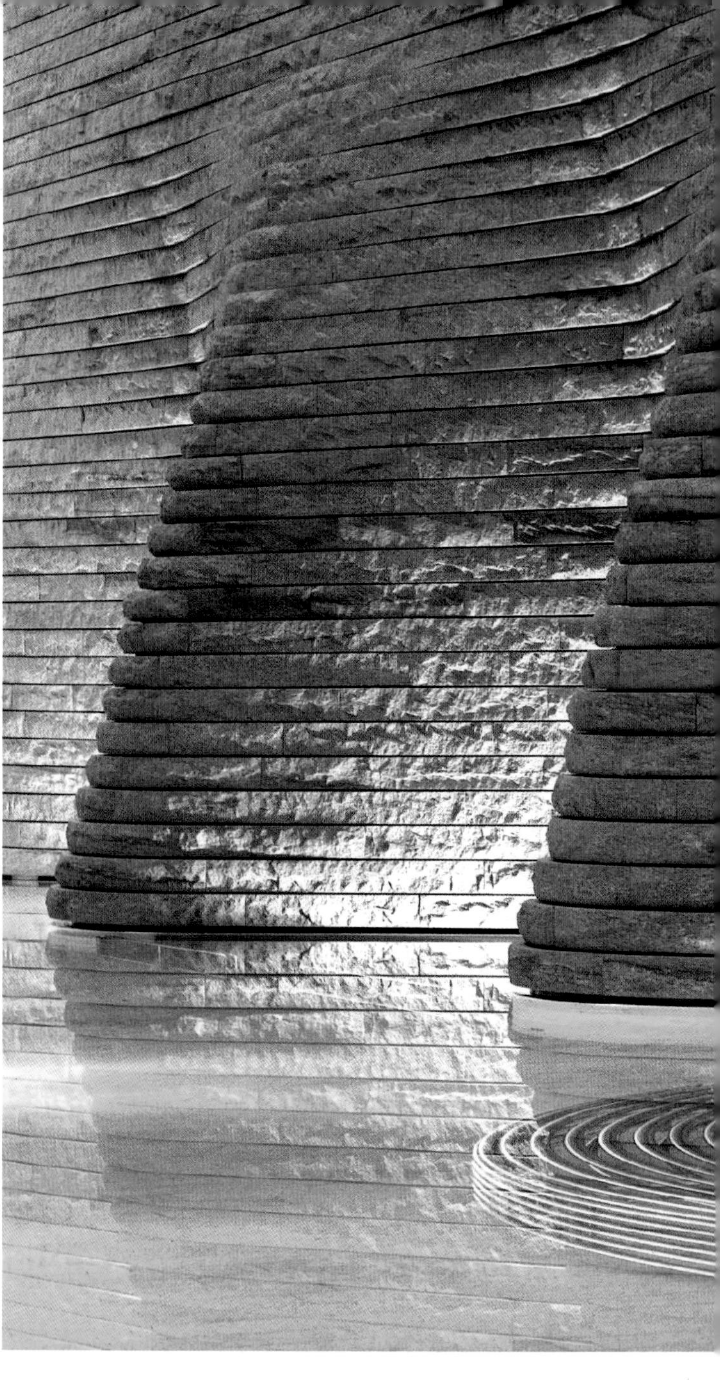

A **natural basin** surrounded by **mountains**

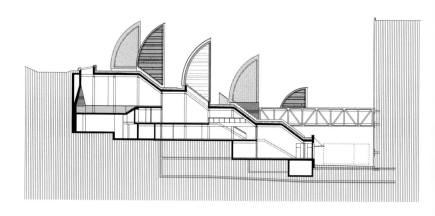

The story-high **green lamellae** create an **introverted ambience**

caldarium
50°C

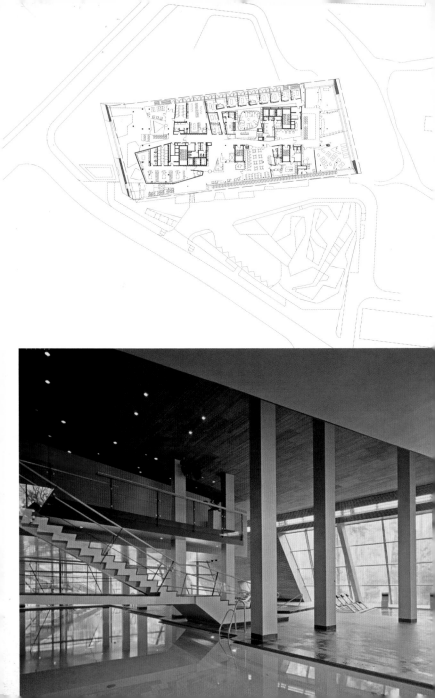

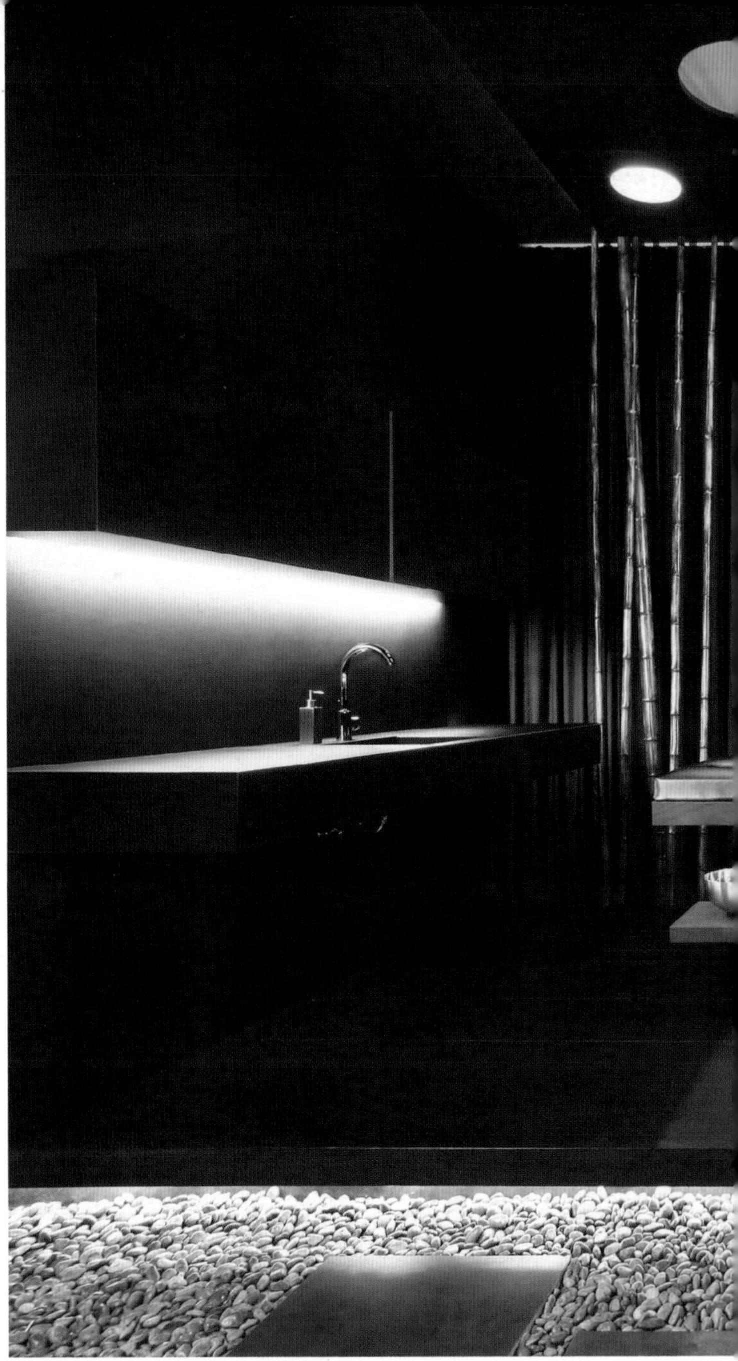

Presenting **holistic lifestyle design** with understated **elegance**

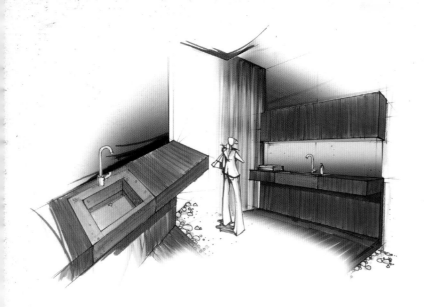

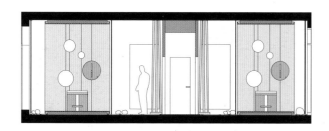

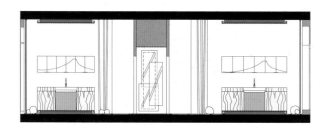

Architects Index

Picture Credits

Barradi, Robert: 166-173
Baumann, Kevin: 314-319
Andrew Bordwin Studio, Inc.: 22-33
Bulot, Antoine: 78-87
Cano, Enrico: 370-375a, 378b
Constantini, Simon, Brixen: 16-21
diephotodesigner.de, Ken
   Schluchtmann, Berlin: 388-397
Eskerod, Torben: 354-367
Ferrero, Alberto: 210-211, 214-218, 220
Christian Gahl: 180-189
Gatkowska, Kasia, Amsterdam: 42-49
Gatto, Marco: 88-97
Genitrini, Arnaldo: 120-121, 123-126,
   128-129
Grobet, Toon: 190-199
hiepler brunier architekturfotografie,
   Berlin: 138-145
Homberger, Urs: 368-369, 375
Kida, Katsuhisa: 236-245
Klazinga, J.: 262-269
Lippens, Evi: 50-57
Knauf, Holger, Düsseldorf: 108-119
Kröger Gross Fotografie: 10-15
KROST, Moskau: 382-383, 386, 387b
Laignel, Eric, New York: 320-327
Lindman, Åke E:son, Stockholm:
   228-229, 233
Lorbach, Marco: 280-285
Marri, Luca: 122, 127
Mørk, Adam: 354-367
Mundt, Helge: 336-345
Powilleit, Inga: 212-213
Popinger, Thomas, Hamburg: 68-77
Reed Business, Doetinchem: 34-41
von Reth, Marc, Hamburg: 246-251

Silverman, James: 226-227, 230-231,
   234-235
Spleth, Jochen, Munich: 98-107,
   270-279
Sobajima, Toshihiro: 346-353
Sunouchi, Motohiro: 152-157
Thoma, Benno: 58-67
Varady, Stephen: 222-225
Wegner, Susanne, Stuttgart: 294-305
Weesterweel, Sebastian: 219- 221
Toshiyuki Yano / Nacasa & Partners
   Inc.: 158-165
Zeljko, Dejan, Zurich: 174-179
Zimmerman, Wade: 146-151

Cover:
Adam Mørk and Torben Eskerod